ASD
Amazing Special & Different

Author David Jacobo
Illustrations by Bannarot S.

Copyright © 2024 by David Jacobo
Illustrations by Bannarot S.

All rights reserved. This book or any portion thereof may not be reproduced or used in any manner whatsoever without the express written permission of the publisher except for the use of brief quotations in a book review.

DEDICATION

Thank you Mom, he is and has always been
a miracle in my life.

Thank you Dariel, for being a little big brother.
Your kindness and selflessness inspires me
to be a better man.

Thank you David Anthony for accomplishing all
obstacles that have been put before you. Thank for making
my life better everyday with your smile and your laughter.

ACKNOWLEDGMENT

Thanks to all of the people that take the time to share a kind word, like hello, or a simple gesture, like a smile, to a child with special-needs. Thank you to all the parents who push through. God sees your efforts.
We are never alone.

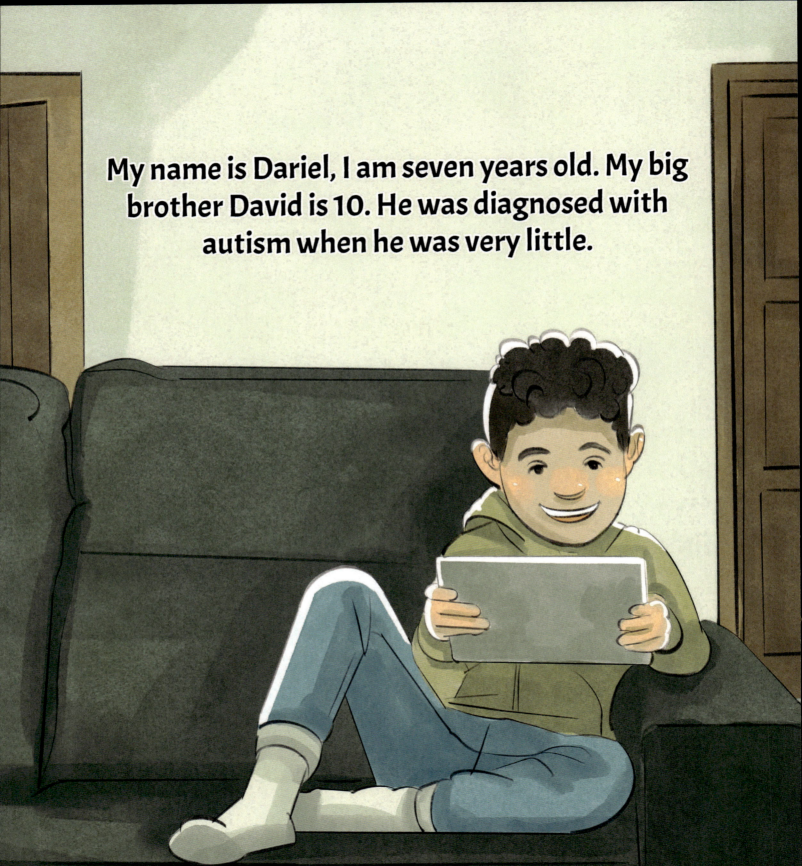

He does things differently than I do at times, and is known for being shy, but he is so cool to me.

My brother David doesn't speak a lot,

My brother David doesn't play with me much,

but he is happy just being around me.

My brother David doesn't like different types of food,

but does share what he likes with me.

My brother David doesn't always look at my face when I speak to him,

but I know he hears every word.

David reads in English, and in Spanish!
He also loves all types of music.

Some people say my brother David is different,

and they are right, he is.

My brother David is AMAZING, SPECIAL, and DIFFERENT. This is why I love him!

ABOUT THE AUTHOR

David Jacobo was born and raised in Washington Heights, New York City. David has had the privilege of being raised by his mother and father and being accompanied by his siblings, a older sister and brother. Living a cultural filled childhood showered with happiness as well as hardships that are accompanied with growing up in an urban neighborhood. David went on to college and got a Masters in special education in early childhood and has been teaching for over 17 years. On July 15, 2012, David was blessed with his second child, David Anthony Jacobo. David Anthony was born with ASD, this changed his father's life forever. At first David felt very upset that he, who dedicate his life to helping children with special needs, was given a child with Autism. It wasn't until he had a conversation with his mother who explained to him that having a child with special needs was a miracle in his life. Even though he did not understand what she said at that moment he understood one thing, that everything was alright and that things will not only get better but reach higher heights and surpass his expectations for his own life. David Jacobo with his experiences as a special education teacher and as a father of a child with special needs knows the importance of teaching acceptance as well as Teaching others to embrace those that are different.

Made in the USA
Middletown, DE
30 March 2025

73489981R00017